# Everything You Need to Know About

# Student-on Student Sexual Harassment

Sexual harassment in school can severely interfere with your ability to concentrate.

# Everything You Need to Know About Student-on Student Sexual Harassment

Debbie Stanley

The Rosen Publishing Group, Inc.
New York

Published in 2000 by The Rosen Publishing Group, Inc.
29 East 21st Street, New York, NY 10010

First Edition

**Library of Congress Cataloging-in-Publication Data**

Stanley, Debbie.
    Everything you need to know about student-on-student sexual harassment / Debbie Stanley.
        p.cm—(The need to know library)
    Includes bibliographical references (p.) and index.
    Summary: Describes sexual harassment of teens by other teens and gives information on how to get help if one is being harassed.
    ISBN 0-8239-3281-8
    1. Sexual harassment in education—United States—Juvenile literature. 2. Teenagers—United States—Sexual behavior—Juvenile literature. [1. Sexual harassment.] I. Series.
LC212.82 .S69 2000
373.15'8—dc21                                              00-025497

*Manufactured in the United States of America*

# Contents

# Introduction

"**H**e's just teasing you because he likes you. If he didn't like you, he would ignore you."

"It's just talk. Kids talk like that—it's no big deal."

"If you don't react, he will lose interest and pick on someone else."

"Don't let it hurt your feelings. Everybody gets called names sometimes."

"Kids are cruel. It'll get better as you get older."

"He's just a bully who is trying to scare you. He's not really going to do anything. Just stay out of his way."

These are just some of the things adults tell kids who complain about being picked on, teased, or threatened.

Adults today grew up hearing these same remarks, and many think that since they got through it, their kids can, too. Unfortunately, in many cases kids can't simply tough it out—they are actually in danger of being physically harmed or emotionally damaged. Luckily, people are beginning to see how much harm can result from intense, ongoing harassment.

One type of harassment that is especially dangerous is sexual harassment. Sexual harassment is hard to define because every situation is different, but in general it means that someone is making unwanted sexual advances or remarks toward you or engaging in sexual conduct around you and it's causing you to be afraid or to limit your life. Both the victim and the harasser can be any age and either gender, but the harasser is someone who has scared the victim by being in a position of power over the victim, by simply being bigger or stronger, or by behaving in a sexually harassing way. Examples include a boss harassing an employee, a teacher harassing a student, or even a student harassing another student.

In order for harassment to be considered sexual, it has to include some sort of sexual conduct. This can be physical contact or remarks about a person's body; suggestions or demands for sex or some other type of intimacy, such as a kiss or a date; the spreading of sexual rumors about a person; or threats that if the harasser doesn't get the contact he or she wants, the victim will suffer in some way, such as being attacked, fired from a job, or given a failing grade in a class. It can also include displaying sexually explicit drawings or pictures, telling dirty jokes or stories, or using sexual gestures.

Some sexual conduct is directed at a certain person, such as spreading rumors about someone or harassing him or her for a date. Other things, such as sexual graffiti or telling dirty jokes, can be done without a specific person as the target and can still be considered sexual harassment. It is also important to note that it doesn't matter whether or not the harasser meant to hurt the victim. If the behavior causes the victim harm, even if the harasser didn't mean it to, it is still sexual harassment.

Sometimes people have a hard time knowing whether physical contact is "sexual in nature." A good way to tell the difference between an innocent touch and a sexual touch is with the "bathing suit" rule: If someone touches you in a place that would be covered by your bathing suit, that may be considered a sexual touch. Kissing and hugging can also be considered sexual contact. It is important to know that there are exceptions, such as contact between athletes when they are training or competing, especially in sports such as wrestling. Sometimes teachers hug students to encourage them or to make them feel better if they are upset or hurt. There is even that habit of male coaches slapping male players on the behind—something that a lot of people find strange but that continues anyway. The most important thing to remember is that if you don't want to be touched, you have the right to say so; if the person keeps touching you, it could be considered sexual harassment.

In this book we will discuss sexual harassment of one student by another. Student sexual harassment is illegal and is covered by a law called Title IX, which is enforced by the U.S. Department of Education's Office for Civil Rights (OCR). You will learn much more about Title IX and the OCR in this book. Much of the information you will find here can also apply to harassment in general or to sexual harassment of a student by an adult or of one adult by another. If you think someone you know is being harassed or if you are being harassed, please talk to someone you trust and get help. You will find more information on how to get help later on in this book.

Sometimes it can be hard to tell if a specific behavior is sexual harassment.

# Chapter One

## What Is Student-on-Student Sexual Harassment?

**I**t can be difficult to know whether or not a certain behavior is sexual harassment. For example, suppose a boy sneaks up behind a girl and pinches her butt. Is that sexual harassment? We can't decide yet because we need more information.

1) We need to know how the girl felt about it. Did she think it was funny or flattering, or was she upset?

2) We need to know who the boy is. Is he her boyfriend or someone she likes? Is he someone she doesn't know? Or is he someone the girl has been trying to avoid all semester?

3) If the contact was unwanted by the girl, we need to know how many times this boy has done similar things to her. Is this the first time, or has it been going on for a while?

4) Finally, we have to know what the girl is going to do because of the boy's contact with her. Will she just ignore it or gather her friends to get revenge on him? Will she tell an adult, or will she perhaps skip school sometimes because she is afraid she will run into that boy?

Since there are so many questions to be answered, it is impossible to simply make a list of things that are always sexual harassment. Let's consider the above four points in more detail.

1) How did the girl feel about the contact? In order for sexual conduct to be considered harassment, it has to be unwelcome or unwanted. The OCR points out that "conduct is unwelcome if the student does not request or invite the conduct, and views it as offensive or undesirable. However, just because a student does not immediately speak out or complain does not mean that the sexual conduct was welcome." This is a very important point. You do not have to speak out against someone else's treatment of

you in order to have a valid complaint. You don't have to "defend yourself" before complaining. As a student, stopping sexual harassment is not your job—it's the school's job to protect you from it.

2) Who is the boy? If he is the girl's boyfriend and she didn't mind the pinch, then there is no sexual harassment. If he is someone whom she doesn't want any contact with, there may be a sexual harassment problem developing.

3) How many times has this happened? The more times a person forces unwanted sexual contact on another person, the more likely it is that the contact will qualify as sexual harassment.

4) How will the girl respond? If the contact was unwanted, the girl was probably bothered by it. She might be able to ignore it the first time, or she might tell him to leave her alone or have a friend talk to him. Some people can brush off a single incident, while others may find it extremely upsetting. If the contact continues, however, the girl will most likely become more and more upset. If the boy's contact with her begins to interfere with her happiness, her ability to study, or her choice of classes or activities, then that boy is most likely guilty of sexual harassment.

## The Three U's

As a general rule, an incident (or series of incidents) can be considered sexual harassment if it meets the three U's:

- Uninvited

- Unwanted

- Uncomfortable

If you think you are being harassed—or even if you are not so sure—you should keep a log of exactly what happens over the course of a few days. Include who was involved and exactly what was said. Likewise, both verbal and nonverbal aspects of harassment should be taken into consideration. Verbal includes teasing; nonverbal includes tone of voice, graffiti, and body language. On the basis of this log, you can decide what to do next.

*I'm going to be a journalist, and so I want to work on the school newspaper. I figure the experience will help me get into the college I want to go to. Jenna, the editor of the paper, promised that she would give me a column if I went out with her. I don't like her that way, but I don't know what to do. I really want the column, and she's the one who makes those decisions.*

There are two categories of sexual harassment. The first is known by the Latin term "quid pro quo," and it is the type of sexual harassment that occurs when one person demands a date or sexual contact from another person in return for something. The reward promised to the victim might be a better grade, a pay raise or promotion, or protection from another threatening person. Sometimes the victims are either told or led to believe that if they don't go along, they will not only not get the reward but they will be punished by being flunked, fired, excluded, or beaten. Since this type of sexual harassment is more direct and specific, it is usually easier to know that it is sexual harassment.

*I hate French class. There's one guy who talks about me and stares at me all the time. Sometimes he comes up behind me and snaps my bra strap. He makes sexual gestures toward me when I have to walk past him to go to the board. One time when I was writing on the board, he said, really loud, that he couldn't wait to get his hands on me. Everybody laughed. I looked over at the teacher, and he was laughing, too!*

The second type of sexual harassment is called hostile environment. A hostile environment is created when the harasser makes the victim extremely uncomfortable in a certain place, such as school. The place is somewhere that the victim has a right to be, or is required to be, and has to go to even though he or she is afraid because of the harasser. The OCR defines hostile environment harassment in schools as "unwelcome sexually harassing conduct [that] is so severe, persistent, or pervasive that it affects a student's ability to participate in or benefit from an education program or activity, or creates an intimidating, threatening, or abusive educational environment." This type of sexual harassment is much more general, so there are many more behaviors that can be classified this way than there are in quid pro quo harassment. However, since this category is so general and broad, it can sometimes be hard to decide whether a situation is actually sexual harassment. The OCR notes that "a hostile environment can be created by a school employee, another student, or even someone visiting the school, such as a student or employee from another school."

It takes only one quid pro quo incident for the harasser to be guilty of sexual harassment, but in most cases it takes a number of incidents over time for a person to be guilty of creating a hostile environment. For example, according to the OCR, "a sexual joke, even if offensive to the student to whom it was told, will not by itself create a sexually hostile environment. However, a sexual assault or other severe single incident can create a hostile environment."

> *There are three girls who terrorize a lot of the other girls at school, but me especially. One girl, Tanya, the leader, really hates me for some reason, and every chance she gets she tells people I'm a slut. I'm not, but now I'm afraid to go out with any guy because of what he might be expecting. They talk about me in class, in the halls . . . they even write stuff on the bathroom walls and in the textbooks that get passed out to other kids the next year. They put stickers on my locker that are hard to peel off. Some of the teachers just look away when Tanya and her friends start talking about me and some have told them to stop, but a few of the teachers look at me as if they're wondering if what they say is true.*

There are at least two "gray areas," or situations in which it is unclear whether sexual harassment is happening. The first is the case of same-sex harassment. For example, if one girl continually calls another girl a slut and causes the victim to be uncomfortable and afraid, that is definitely harassment of some sort. Since it involves sexual remarks, does that make it sexual harassment?

17

No. 97-843

In the
Supreme Court of the United States
October Term, 1998

---

**AURELIA DAVIS, as next friend of LaSHONDA D.,**
*Petitioner,*

v.

**MONROE COUNTY BOARD OF EDUCATION, et al.,**
*Respondent*

---

On Writ of *Certiorari* to
United States Court of Appeals for the Eleventh Circuit

**BRIEF *AMICUS CURIAE* OF THE
AMERICAN CIVIL LIBERTIES
UNION AND THE ACLU OF
GEORGIA IN SUPPORT OF
PETITIONER**

Sexual harassment is a crime, and many lawsuits have been filed on behalf of harassed students.

*I had a friend who decided to be brave and let everyone know he was gay. He said he thought the world was "evolved enough" for him to be able to come out, and he thought it would help other gay students to have the courage to come forward, too. Well, it didn't work. He got jumped in the locker room after gym class one day, and they beat him up so bad he was unconscious. His family had to move away so he could finish school somewhere where nobody knew him.*

Another gray area involves homosexuals who are harassed because of their sexual orientation. While it is obvious that there is a sexual element to the harassment, it is sometimes identified not as sexual harassment but as a hate crime. This makes a difference in what can be done to the harasser to stop or punish him or her.

Both of these gray areas involve same-sex sexual harassment. The OCR makes it clear that Title IX protects "both male and female students from sexual harassment, regardless of who the harasser is." Still, some people have tried to find loopholes in the law by claiming that the harassment was not actually sexual harassment.

Sexual harassment is illegal. No matter who the harasser is and who the victim is, schools are obligated

Young gays and lesbians are often harassed because of their sexual orientation.

to protect their students from sexual harassment. A gray area in the law does not take away your rights to study, work, and feel safe. There are occasions, however, when a school administrator may not give your case as much attention as it requires. If that should happen, don't lose hope. Help is available for you.

We will discuss Title IX in more detail in chapter 3, but first, let's look at what sexual harassment does to the victim.

# Chapter Two

# What It Does to the Victim

*I don't get it. What's the big deal? All I did was ask her out a few times, and she got so uptight, I couldn't help making fun of her for it. Can't she take a joke? I mean, man, she's such a stress case. What does she think I'm gonna do, rape her or something?*

While it may seem like harmless teasing to some people, sexual harassment can have permanent, serious effects on the victims. Sexual harassment is psychological torture. It causes the victim to feel afraid, nervous, and hesitant about things that were once no problem. It changes victims' lives and cheats them out of happiness, fun, and peace of mind. "As a result of sexual harassment," the OCR reports, "a student may . . . have trouble learning, drop a class or drop out of school altogether, lose trust in school officials, become isolated, fear for personal safety, or lose self-esteem."

What are victims of sexual harassment afraid of? It could be the embarrassment of being targeted and made fun of in front of other kids. It could be that the victim hates the way it feels to be disrespected. Perhaps the victim is sad because his or her friends and teachers aren't doing anything to help. It could be that the victim is afraid of the threat of physical violence, even rape. Even if the harasser didn't intend to be threatening, that is how such behavior is often interpreted. Studies have shown that many victims of sexual harassment say they don't want to go to school anymore, they don't want to talk as much in class, they find it harder to pay attention in school, or they want to change schools. More than half report feeling embarrassed or self-conscious because of the harassment, and some are less self-assured, less confident, and doubtful that they'll be able to have a happy romantic relationship.

## Missing Out on Learning

*When I look back on my last semester of high school, all I remember is the constant fear. I had been a good student up until then, but the last thing on my mind during that time was my*

Victims of sexual harassment often avoid going to school after the incident.

*grades. I just wanted to get through school and get out so I wouldn't have to be afraid anymore. If I had kept my grade point average up, I probably would have gotten a scholarship for college, but I just couldn't handle it. So I got a job, figuring I'd work for a year, save some money, and then go to college. It has been five years and I just haven't gotten around to it yet.*

When sexual harassment happens in school, the victim begins to dread going and may even skip certain classes or whole days of school just to keep from being harassed. The victim loses out on a full education because he or she either doesn't go to classes or is too nervous to relax and concentrate on learning. "A . . . student should feel safe and comfortable walking down the halls of his or her school," say Nan Stein and Lisa Sjostrom in their book *Flirting or Hurting? A Teacher's Guide to Student-on-Student Sexual Harassment in Schools.* "School is a place for learning and growing. Sexual harassment stops that process."

## Avoiding Social Situations

*People can't believe that I never went to a high school dance. My friends now look at my school pictures and say, "You were pretty! What did you have to hide?" The truth is, I spent four years running from one person, the same person who had tormented me in junior high. He kept it up in high school, and he had a lot of friends who joined in, too. It was bad enough listening to their lewd comments in class; I couldn't stand the thought of dealing with it outside of school, too.*

Someone who is the victim of sexual harassment might be afraid to go to school dances, plays, or games because the harasser might be there. The victim might have made new friends at these events, friends who could have helped him or her to deal with the harassment, but the fear of further run-ins with the harasser keeps the victim home.

24

## Loss of Self-Esteem

*I used to love school, and I think I liked myself, too. I don't remember feeling like a failure back in the second or third grade. Now that I'm in seventh grade, I hate school. I hate this place. I hate these people. Nobody cares about what the other kids do to me. Nobody helps me. I guess I'm not worth it.*

There's an old saying: "If you tell someone they're bad often enough, eventually they'll start to believe it." This is especially true of children, who haven't lived long enough or had enough experience to know that they are good and worthy of love and respect. Kids pretty much go by what their parents, teachers, and friends tell them—and don't tell them. If a kid has parents who don't know how to express love, teachers who don't care, or classmates who make fun of them, that kid will probably have low self-esteem. If a kid has loving parents and encouraging teachers, he or she may be able to get over teasing from other kids when it happens.

The same is true of a person who is the victim of sexual harassment. Being constantly harassed and feeling powerless to do anything about it can be damaging to a person's confidence and self-image. If the victim has someone to turn to for help, the damage can

Sexual harassment can do serious damage to your self-esteem.

be kept to a minimum; if the victim doesn't know that help is available or doesn't know where to go to get it, the harassment will probably keep wearing away the victim's self-esteem.

## Damage to Relationships

*This kid at school keeps talking dirty to me. I told my mother, and she got all embarrassed and walked away. She acted as if I should be embarrassed, too. I tried talking to my sister, and she laughed and said I should just ignore it. I even asked my older brother to help me, but he said I should learn to fight my own battles. Some family— I can't count on any of them, that's for sure.*

If a person can't discuss his or her problems with a friend or parent, the relationship will suffer. This can happen when a person is the victim of sexual harassment. If a child tells a parent or older sibling that he or she is being harassed in school and the older person brushes it off by saying it happens to everyone and to just ignore it, the child may feel that his or her fears aren't important. This will make it harder for the child to go to his or her family with a problem the next time.

The same can happen with friends. If our friends don't take our fears and worries seriously, we begin

When friends don't take your fears and concerns seriously, you may think that they don't care.

to think they don't care. They probably just don't understand, but that doesn't help when what we need is someone to back us up and help find a solution.

If a victim of sexual harassment is so afraid that he or she begins to avoid social situations, friends might misinterpret this and think the victim doesn't want to be their friend anymore. If a person turns down an invitation to a party or says no to someone who wants to take them on a date or to a dance, the other person isn't likely to say, "Oh, it's probably not because of me." Most people will take it personally and assume he or she just doesn't want to be with them.

Over time, sexual harassment and the victim's reaction to it can cause the victim to lose friends, alienate family members, and gain a reputation as a person who doesn't want to do anything or see anyone.

## Emotional Disorders

### Depression

*I sleep a lot now. I used to enjoy reading, even the stuff we have to do for school, but now I'm just not interested in it. My parents keep accusing me of having anorexia because I don't eat much anymore, but nothing tastes good. I just don't feel like eating. I don't really feel like doing anything.*

Depression is a serious disorder in which the victim feels hopeless, sad, and unmotivated, and loses interest in

29

Harassment can cause severe anxiety in the form of panic attacks or nightmares.

things such as doing well in school, excelling at a sport or hobby, or being with friends. People who no longer want to do things that they used to enjoy may be suffering from depression. They may say they just don't care about those things anymore or that there's no point in trying because they won't do well anyway. Depression can be caused by problems such as being the victim of sexual harassment. There are treatments for depression, including medications, but unless the root cause of the depression is taken care of, the depression can't really be cured.

## Anxiety

*I have so many nightmares now! I jump when I hear the slightest noise. People laugh at that.*

*Sometimes I know why I'm nervous—it's because of school—but sometimes I feel really scared and I don't even know why.*

Anxiety is kind of the opposite of depression. Instead of being down in the dumps and sad, the person is nervous, high-strung, and jittery most of the time. Some people even have panic attacks, frightening episodes in which they feel intense fear and may even think they're about to die.

Another possibility is that the victim may develop a phobia, or intense fear, of things such as being in public or being around other people. Phobias can be disabling because they keep the person from being able to do the things we all have to do in life, such as working or going to the grocery store. Phobias also keep the victim from being able to enjoy fun things such as going to the movies or to parties. Once a fear has progressed into a phobia, it is very difficult to cure it by yourself. You can't just talk yourself out of it.

Many psychologists believe that phobias begin with a very bad, very scary experience; they are your mind's way of trying to protect you from the thing you fear, even if the original danger is past and the fear is now irrational. An irrational fear is one that doesn't make sense because the thing you're afraid of isn't likely to hurt you. For example, some people are afraid of crowds, perhaps because they were lost in a crowd once

Sometimes people overeat to cope with emotional stress.

when they were younger. As a child, being lost in a crowd is scary and dangerous; as an adult, being in a crowd is not nearly as dangerous and is sometimes necessary in everyday life. So a phobia of being surrounded by other people is very limiting for the victim.

If phobias are triggered by a very scary experience, then sexual harassment could cause a large number of them. The victim could become intensely afraid of:

- Places that are like the ones they've been victimized in, such as schools, buses, hallways, or bathrooms

- Any small or confined space, such as a closed office or a car (this is called claustrophobia)

- Situations that remind them of the harassment, such as going to college, dating, studying with others, or participating in sports or school plays

- People who look like their harasser, or who are the same gender, or who wear the same cologne or clothing

- Authority figures, or people who have some sort of power over them, including teachers, bosses, counselors, or the police

If a person is frightened and terrorized enough by the experience of being sexually harassed, there's no telling how bad the psychological damage could be or how it might show up later in the victim's life.

## Eating Disorders

*I have a friend who does nothing but eat. It's amazing how much she can eat. Sometimes I go to her house to do homework or to watch TV, and I just can't believe all the food she goes through in one afternoon. I would have a stomachache for sure. I worry about her because she seems unhappy a lot of the time, and I don't think the eating is helping.*

Both boys and girls can develop eating disorders in response to problems in their lives. Some doctors and researchers believe that eating disorders, such as anorexia, bulimia, and binge eating disorder, can be caused by such things as physical, emotional, or sexual abuse; tension at home, such as parents who fight a lot; or anything that causes the victim to feel that he or she has no control over his or her own life. This theory says that the eating disorder is an attempt by the victim to take back some control. Others say that being teased or picked on for being overweight can lead to disordered eating as a desperate attempt by the victim to change his or her body and stop the teasing. If these theories are correct, then it makes sense that sexual harassment could trigger an eating disorder.

## Suicide or Murder

*There was a kid in our school who everybody picked on. He was small and the bigger boys would beat up on him all the time. Some of the girls did, too. He transferred to another school a few years ago, and they say he got really big and really mean. Now there's a rumor that he's coming after the kids in my school who picked on him when he was here.*

Unfortunately, there have been many cases of young people who struck back after years of being teased, bullied, or harassed. Some ended the misery by killing themselves, sometimes right in front of their class-mates, and others finally cracked and killed not only

34

those they believed had hurt them but other innocent people as well. Some people believe that in many cases, the students who go into a school and shoot their classmates are the ones who have been picked on relentlessly and finally come to see no other solution.

Sexual harassment and all forms of bullying should be taken seriously and should be prevented as much as possible because they can do a lot of damage to the victims. Still, no matter how mean and evil the harasser is, he or she does not deserve to be killed for it. Schools, parents, and kids themselves need to know how to deal with harassment before it becomes so severe that it drives a student to such extreme measures.

There are so many bad things that can happen as a result of sexual harassment. Now that society is beginning to recognize the potential damage sexual harassment can cause, people are starting to see it as more than just kids being kids. For this reason, sexual harassment is against the law.

Phobias can make people uncomfortable with social situations.

# Chapter Three

# What the Law Says

**M**any schools have developed rules and guidelines telling students what their rights are and how to respect the rights of others. The schools often include a discussion of sexual harassment in these guidelines. Public schools are required by law to have a sexual harassment policy and to inform students, parents, and teachers about it. If there is a report of sexual harassment, the school is required by law to investigate and to make the harasser stop. If the school knows there is a problem and does not protect the victim, it is in violation of Title IX.

Title IX prohibits sex discrimination, which includes sexual harassment. It was passed as part of the Education Amendments of 1972, so sexual harassment has been illegal for a long time. Unfortunately, it hasn't always been taken seriously, especially in schools. That is starting to change now. The Office for Civil Rights, part of the U.S. Department of Education, is in charge of making sure people know about Title IX. According to the OCR, sexual harassment is often "allowed to continue simply because students and employees are not informed about what sexual harassment is or how to stop it." The OCR published a document called *Sexual Harassment Guidance* in 1997 to make the problem clearer to everyone.

## What Title IX Says

Title IX clarifies a lot of things, but the OCR makes it even easier to understand through publications such as the *Sexual Harassment Guidance* and *Sexual Harassment: It's Not Academic*, a discussion of Title IX available on the OCR Web site (see Where to Go for Help at the back of this book). Some of the questions answered by Title IX and the OCR include the following:

*Who can be a victim of sexual harassment? Is it only girls? Do you have to be younger than the harasser?*

The OCR reports that sexual harassment "can affect any student, regardless of sex, race, or age."

*If you're a student being harassed by another student, but it's not on school grounds, does the school have to stop it?*

Sometimes. The OCR says, "Sexual harassment can occur at any school activity and can take place in classrooms, halls, cafeterias, dormitories, and other areas." So even if you're miles from the school on a ski trip or at a track meet, you are still protected from sexual harassment because those are school events. "Title IX protects students from unlawful sexual harassment in all of a school's programs or activities, whether they take place in the facilities of the school, on a school bus, at a class or training program sponsored by the school at another location, or elsewhere," says the OCR. So even field trips are covered.

*I've never heard of my school having a rule against sexual harassment. Do they have to have one?*

If your school receives federal funding, then yes, it has to have a sexual harassment policy. According to the OCR, "Under federal law, a school is required to have a policy against sex discrimination and notify employees, students, and elementary and secondary school parents of the policy." If you go to a private school, you can still demand that it make up a sexual harassment policy, based on all of the important points that led to Title IX. Private schools count on tuition and donations from former students to keep running. If enough current and past students get angry with the school, it will lose money. So it is in every school's best interest to have a sexual harassment policy.

Besides having a policy against sexual harassment and making sure that all students and employees of the school know about it, schools are also required to have a procedure for students to complain if sexual harassment does occur. Students should know that they have a right to ask for help and that it is illegal for anyone to take revenge on them for speaking up.

*Does Title IX say who I'm supposed to talk to if someone is harassing me?*

Title IX requires schools to have at least one employee who is in charge of making sure the school meets all the requirements of the law. This does not mean, though, that you have to find out who that person is and talk to them if you have a problem. But you do have to tell someone in order to get the school's help.

One important thing to understand about Title IX is that it says the school must be told about the harassment. The school can't be expected to just know about it. This puts some responsibility on the victim. Sometimes another person may see the harassment and report it, but usually the victim has to tell someone about it. There have been many disputes over who should be told. In some cases, a student told a teacher or a school nurse, and that person did nothing about the harassment. The school argued that it could not be held responsible because the victim hadn't told the right person. In most schools, however, any adult who has contact with students, including teachers, coaches, counselors, and nurses, can be told about harassment and must pass the information on to whoever is in charge so that it can be stopped. A student can also tell his or her parents and have them report it to the school. The law puts the burden on the school to make sure all of its employees follow up on sexual harassment claims, rather than requiring students to know who to talk to or making them talk to a certain person.

*I went out with this girl one time, and now she won't leave me alone. She leaves sappy notes in my locker, and she keeps making up stories about stuff we supposedly did together, sexual stuff. One time she came up to me in the cafeteria and sat in my lap! I'm really sick of it, but maybe it's my fault because I went out with her that one time.*

You don't have to put up with unwanted attention, even if you accepted it willingly in the past or did not immediately speak out against it. According to the OCR, "A student might feel that objecting would only result in increasing the harassing conduct." Sometimes, students feel intimidated by the conduct and/or feel too embarrassed, confused, or fearful to complain or resist.

You don't have to accept unwanted attention, even if it did not bother you in the past.

Also, a student who willingly participates in conduct on one occasion may later decide that the same conduct on a subsequent occasion has become unwelcome." So even if "you liked it the first time," or "you didn't complain the first time," as some harassers might say, that doesn't mean you can't complain now.

## Problems with Enforcement of Title IX

Title IX was an important step toward preventing sexual harassment, and it is strong in many ways. Still, there are some problems that make it less than perfect. Below are some of the limitations of Title IX.

Some people believe they should be allowed to say whatever they want because the Constitution gives them the right to free speech. However, if their free speech violates another person's right to be free from harassment, someone has to decide whose rights are more important. Schools are encouraged to settle such disputes themselves, but sometimes the decision has to be made in court. If a person accused of sexual harassment can prove that what he or she said qualifies as "protected speech," then the harassment case against him or her probably won't stand. An example might be a student who says, over and over, that women are not as good as men, that men are smarter and more important, and that women should do whatever men tell them to do because that's what his religion says. The student might demand a date with a girl and refuse to leave her alone when she says no. If the girl accuses him of sexual harassment, he could respond by claiming that he was simply exercising his right to express his religious beliefs.

Things get more complicated when a victim of sexual harassment doesn't want the harasser to know who told. When a victim wants to be anonymous, it can be difficult for the school. Suppose the principal pulls the harasser out of class in order to ask him or her about the victim's claims. Instead of saying "Shelly Jones says you have been grabbing her and sending her obscene notes," because the principal doesn't want to identify the victim, he or she would only be able to say something like "I've gotten a complaint about you bothering another student." This is, obviously, much easier to deny, and it's so vague that the harasser could easily protest whatever punishment he or she receives.

Another problem is that Title IX applies only to schools that receive federal funds. This includes public schools, but it could mean that some private schools are technically not required to follow Title IX. However, since sexual harassment is such a serious problem, it makes sense for every school to have a policy against it, whether the school has to or not. The OCR makes it very clear that schools should prevent sexual harassment to protect students from harm, not just to protect themselves from lawsuits: "A school should not accept, tolerate, or overlook sexual harassment. A school should not excuse the harassment with an attitude of 'that's just emerging adolescent sexuality' or 'boys will be boys,' or ignore it for fear of damaging a professor's reputation. This does nothing to stop the sexual harassment and can even send a message that such conduct is accepted or tolerated by the school." If a school works to prevent sexual harassment before it starts, the OCR says, the result is an even stronger learning environment: "When a school makes it clear that sexual harassment will not be tolerated, trains its staff, and appropriately responds when harassment occurs, students will see the school as a safe place where everyone can learn."

# Chapter Four

# Preventing and Stopping Sexual Harassment

**T**here is no surefire way to keep sexual harassment from happening, but there are a lot of things that schools, students, and parents can do to try to prevent it or to stop it when it does happen.

## What Schools Can Do

Schools have a responsibility to keep their students safe from harm. Even if they are not legally required to prevent sexual harassment, they have a moral obligation to do so. The first step is to develop rules about sexual harassment. "A policy against sex discrimination, particularly one that specifically addresses sexual harassment, is an extremely important method for preventing sexual harassment," says the OCR. "Such a policy lets students, parents, and employees know that sexual harassment will not be tolerated." The policy should include:

- A clear definition of sexual harassment, with examples of unacceptable behavior.

- An explanation of how to make a complaint, including who to write or talk to and what that person will do with the information.

- A promise to take all complaints seriously and to follow through with punishment if sexual harassment does occur.

- A discussion of what that punishment will be.

- A warning that retaliation or revenge against the person complaining will also be punished.

- Information on contacting the OCR or other source for assistance outside the school if needed.

Once the policy is written, it must be distributed to all employees and students of the school and sent home to parents, so everyone knows about it and knows what is expected of them. If an incident does occur, the school must take action to stop it, to punish the harasser, and to prevent future incidents. If the school has a policy in place but doesn't act on it when the time comes, the policy is useless.

In addition to creating a sexual harassment policy, schools should make it clear to their employees that any

School sexual harassment policies should be understood by both students and their parents.

hint of sexual harassment, whether it comes from an actual student complaint or is witnessed by the employee, should not be ignored. All school employees should be made aware of the seriousness of sexual harassment and should be held accountable for preventing or stopping it. Some additional recommendations from the OCR include age-appropriate sexual harassment awareness training for students, separate training for school staff and/or parents, and surveying of students to find out if sexual harassment is happening.

## How Parents Can Help

Parents should be aware that sexual harassment can happen to their children no matter what age or gender they are. They should find out whether their kids' schools have a sexual harassment policy, and if they don't, parents should get involved and demand that one be written and enforced.

Even if a policy is in place, parents should know that harassment can still occur. They should watch for signs such as a change in attitude, drop in grades, fear of school, or withdrawal from school-related activities. These changes might not indicate that the child is being sexually harassed, but they probably are the result of some sort of problem with which the child needs help.

## How Students Can Help Themselves

Don't be afraid to ask for help if someone is harassing you. You have a right to go to school without being afraid, worried, anxious, or nervous about what some-one else is going to do to you. Talk to someone you trust—a teacher, coach, or counselor, for example—and if that person doesn't do something about it, talk to someone else. Tell your parents, too, and ask them to help you make sure the school stands up for your rights.

## Write It Down

Remember to write down any incident of harassment that happens to you. This will be very valuable when you need to tell an adult what is happening. Include the date, the time, the location, and what was said.

It might also help to develop an assertive attitude. This means that you present yourself as a confident person who won't tolerate being pushed around. It doesn't mean you have to be rude or aggressive all the time. It just means that you are very clear about what is acceptable to you and what is not.

If someone asks you out and you don't want to go, politely say, "No, thanks." If the person persists, be firm: "I said no, thank you. I don't want to go out with you." You don't have to give a reason. This can sometimes end the problem before it starts because some people think that if you don't say anything, you're not sure, and if they keep bugging you they might get what they want. If you are very clear, they might leave you alone. Remember not to be rude, though. Be calm but firm.

The same technique can be used if someone tells a joke that offends you. If it's important enough to you to speak up, you can simply say, "That offends me. Please don't tell me jokes like that." You don't have to shout or sound angry. If the person didn't mean to offend you, and you point it out in a calm way that doesn't embarrass him or her, he or she will probably apologize and remember not to talk that way around you next time.

If someone is bothering you with sexual conduct and you want to confront him or her, make sure you can do so safely. If you have any worries at all that the person might become violent, don't do it. But if you think

49

An assertive attitude shows very clearly what is unacceptable to you.

you can handle the problem yourself, use the same assertiveness technique: Tell him or her to stop and say what it is you want him or her to stop doing. Be firm but not rude. Say that if he or she doesn't stop, you will report it. If other people hear you and start to laugh, don't let it bother you. They're laughing at the situation, not at you. Even if they do make fun of you for standing up for yourself, they will ultimately respect you for it.

Remember, though, you don't have to confront a person who is harassing you. You can go to an adult, either your parents or someone in school, and let them deal with it for you. That's their job. And never, ever confront someone who has threatened you with violence. If

## If You or a Friend Is Being Harassed

If you are being harassed:

- Say "Stop!"
- Ask for help.
- Don't delay.
- Write it down.

If you are a bystander:

- Don't laugh.
- Be supportive of your friend.
- Go with your friend to ask for help.
- Take notes.

you fight with them, you're likely to get hurt and get into trouble yourself, and it won't solve the problem. Go to an adult who can protect you from that person.

If you are a victim of sexual harassment and you've experienced any of the problems discussed in chapter 2, such as depression, anxiety, isolation, or any other negative effects, talk to someone about it. You may need help to get over these problems, even after the harassment stops. Talking to a counselor or your parents can help you deal with the lingering pain of being victimized. You may also want to talk to a professional, such as a psychologist, who can help you get past the bad experience and move on with your life.

# Bad Advice

Here are some examples of what not to do in response to sexual harassment:

- "Just ignore it." According to the OCR, "Harassing behavior, if ignored or not reported, is likely to continue and become worse, rather than go away." You may not want to make a big deal out of it, but if the harassing behavior has been going on for a while and it's really bothering you, you owe it to yourself to do something about it.

- "Tell him if he doesn't leave you alone, he'll be sorry." Making vague threats like this will not stop the problem and may make it worse. If you choose to confront the harasser, follow the suggestions above and avoid using threatening or harassing behavior of your own.

- "Give her a taste of her own medicine." Retaliating by trying to scare or embarrass the other person probably won't end the problem and might get you in trouble. Getting revenge might feel good, but in the long run, it won't help the harasser to see why he or she was wrong and make him or her want to change; instead, it will probably just make the harasser more angry, more bitter, and more likely to pick on someone else.

Making vague threats to a harasser rarely solves the problem.

◆ "Just stay away from them." Limiting your life to avoid running into people who are harassing you is no way to live. If someone else's behavior is so disturbing that you don't want to go to school, or you want to change classes because of it, it's time to get help. You shouldn't have to change your plans and be miserable because someone else is victimizing you.

# Are You Guilty of Sexual Harassment?

If you have read this far, you have a good understanding of what sexual harassment does to the victim, what can happen to the harasser, and what to do if you are harassed. But have you considered the possibility that you yourself could be a harasser? Ask yourself the following questions, keeping in mind that harassers can be male or female:

◆ Are people afraid of me, even if I don't mean to scare them?

◆ Do I pick on people who are smaller or weaker than I am just because they are smaller or weaker?

◆ Do I get into physical fights a lot?

◆ When I ask someone out, do they seem afraid to say no? If they do say no, do I accept it or do I keep asking?

- ◆ Do I tell dirty jokes, swear a lot, or use obscene gestures?

- ◆ Do people blush when they hear me talking? Do I enjoy embarrassing them?

- ◆ Do I ever grab people just to see them jump?

- ◆ Do I feel like I could corner someone and keep them from getting away? Do I ever do it?

- ◆ Have I ever been called a bully? Do I like having that reputation?

Remember the discussion in chapter 2 about what sexual harassment victims are afraid of? Maybe you've been lucky and no one has ever made you feel afraid or embarrassed or defenseless. If so, you probably can't imagine what it feels like. If you think hard, though, you can probably think of a time when someone bigger or stronger than you made you afraid. Maybe you've worked hard to build a reputation as the kid who can take anybody and who isn't afraid of anything, but try to remember what it was like when you were smaller, weaker, and frightened. You decided you didn't want anyone to make you feel that way because it hurt. Now you have to be a bigger, stronger person on the inside, not just the outside, and learn not to victimize those you think are weaker than you.

# Conclusion

Bullying in general is receiving more attention and is now seen as a real threat to students' well-being. Bullying can be considered sexual harassment under certain circumstances. Sexual harassment is against the law, and schools receiving federal funding are legally required to protect students from it. If you believe you are being sexually harassed, please get help. Talk to a trusted adult and ask for help. Remember that your school is obligated to protect you if the harassment is happening in school or at a school event.

   If you have a friend who is being harassed, try to help. Share this book with your friend and show him or her that there are alternatives. If you see someone being harassed, even if it's not a friend of yours, tell someone. Send an anonymous note to the principal if you don't want to be identified. Do what you can to prevent sexual harassment because no one deserves to live in fear.

# Glossary

**assertive**  Bold, confident. A person who speaks up for himself or herself is assertive.

**bully**  A person who is mean or abusive to others who are weaker than he or she is.

**claustrophobia**  An intense fear of enclosed or small spaces.

**discrimination**  To give one group of people fewer advantages because of a characteristic such as their race or gender.

**harass**  To bother, annoy, or frighten, usually repeatedly over a period of time.

**hostile environment**  The type of sexual harassment in which the harasser has created an uncomfortable atmosphere in which the victim is forced to exist. A place where the victim must or wants to be on a regular basis, such as school, it is made hostile because of the harasser's behavior.

**panic attack**   An episode of intense fear, often with no apparent cause. The victim might have a rapid heartbeat, sweating, nausea, and an uncontrollable urge to run away or hide. The victim might even believe that he or she is going to die.

**peer**   A person in the same group or of the same standing as another person. Students in the same grade are considered peers, for example.

**phobia**   An intense fear or inability to tolerate something. For example, people who are extremely afraid of spiders have arachnophobia.

**quid pro quo**   A Latin term meaning "something for something." Quid pro quo is a type of sexual harassment in which the harasser forces the victim to submit to sexual contact in order to keep from being hurt.

**self-esteem**   Confidence and satisfaction with oneself; self-respect.

**sexual harassment**   Harassment involving sexual conduct.

**Title IX**   The law prohibiting the sexual harassment of students.

# Where to Go for Help

## In the United States

FutureWAVE
105 Camino Teresa
Santa Fe, NM 87505
(505) 982-8882
e-mail: future@bullyproof.org
Web site: http://www.bullyproof.org
Offers the "Bullyproof Program," which teaches children how to deal with conflict and violence.

U.S. Department of Education Office for Civil Rights
Mary E. Switzer Building
330 C Street SW
Washington, DC 20202
(800) 421-3481

e-mail: OCR@ed.gov

Web site: http://www.ed.gov/offices/OCR

The Office for Civil Rights enforces Title IX and offers many resources for students, parents, and schools to help them deal with sexual harassment. Each state has a local OCR office that can provide assistance with filing sexual harassment claims.

## In Canada

Canadian Civil Liberties Association

229 Yonge Street, Suite 403

Toronto, ON M5B 1N9

(416) 363-0321

e-mail: ccla@ilap.com

Web site: http://www.ccla.org/index.shtml

## Web Sites

Sexual Assault Information Page

Web site: http://www.cs.utk.edu/~bartley/saInfoPage.html

United States Office for Civil Rights

www.ed.gov/offices/OCR/sexhar00.html

Visit this site to obtain a copy of *Sexual Harassment Guidance: Harassment of Students by School Employees, Other Students, or Third Parties.*

# For Further Reading

Larkin, June. *Sexual Harassment: High School Girls Speak Out.* New York: Second Story Press, 1994.

Morris, B., J. Terpstra, B. Croninger, and E. Linn. *Tune In to Your Rights: A Guide for Teenagers About Turning Off Sexual Harassment.* Ann Arbor, MI: University of Michigan Press, 1985.

Sabella, R. A., and R. D. Myrick. *Confronting Sexual Harassment: Learning Activities for Teens.* New York: Educational Media Corporation, 1995.

Shoop, R. J., and D. L. Edwards. *How to Stop Sexual Harassment in Our Schools: A Handbook and Curriculum Guide for Administrators and Teachers.* New York: Paramount Publishing, 1994.

Stein, Nan. *Classrooms and Courtrooms: Facing Sexual Harassment in K–12 Schools.* New York: Teachers College Press, 1999.

Stein, Nan, and Lisa Sjostrom. *Flirting or Hurting? A Teacher's Guide to Student-on-Student Sexual Harassment in Schools.* New York: National Education Association, 1994.

Strauss, S. *Sexual Harassment and Teens: A Program for Positive Change.* Minneapolis, MN: Free Spirit Publishing, 1992.

# Index

## About the Author

Debbie Stanley has a bachelor's degree in journalism and a master's degree in industrial and organizational psychology.

## Photo Credits

Cover by Maura Boruchow. All interior shots by Maura Boruchow except p. 2 by Ethan Zindler and pp. 23, 26 by Shalhevet Moshe.

## Layout

Geri Giordano